CASH and the Couple:
A New Couple's Guide to Money Management

Visit www.booksurge.com to order additional copies.

CASH and the Couple: A New Couple's Guide to Money Management

Written by MaryAnn Nusom Haverstock, M.S., M.B.A
Edited lovingly by Dan Haverstock, M.S.
Edited critically by Barbara Beliveau, Ph.D. and
MaryBeth McManus, M.S.

2007

CASH and the Couple:
A New Couple's Guide to Money Management

TABLE OF CONTENTS

FOREWORD

Finance is about money. And make no mistake about it, money is a personal subject. We all manage our money differently and we all believe we are managing our money the best way for our personal financial goals to be met. Enter a union of two people who manage the same money in different ways, and each person believes he or she is managing the money the right way to get to the right financial goals. It's no wonder so many divorces are attributed to financial issues that the two individuals could not resolve. This book offers help toward better communicating your financial thoughts to each other as you both move comfortably into a long successful partnership.

The basic questions on this book can be answered as follows:
- **WHO SHOULD BE READING THIS BOOK?** New couples who plan on sharing the majority of their financial plans are the target audience for this book. However, this book is a guidance document for any couple who hasn't quite hit the realization that a couple's financial management approach relies on agreement from both parties on almost all decisions. This often includes those couples who have chosen to have separate finances.
  Previously, people may have been managing their money on their own, and making sole decisions for the management of their money. Now there are two people. Let the games begin! Or at least the negotiations. And that is who reads this book: people who would like someone to moderate their discussions about money.
  This book encourages communication for couples who don't know how to talk about finances. Don't fear the money topic and don't bury the money topic among all the other issues you have to work on as a couple. Talk about money openly. This book encourages partners to show frustration when you cannot agree on a financial decision, and to show victory when you have made joint successful financial decisions. Everyone who reads this book should remember that all of our financial decisions have very personal histories. This book acts as a type of moderator to bring out the questions, bring out the discussion topics, and fizzle out the fights.

- **WHAT TYPE OF INFORMATION WILL I GET OUT OF THIS BOOK?** You'll get financial management questions for you to discuss as a couple, topics for serious financial discussions, and brief lessons on money management theories. Don't think you'll find the latest list of Ph.D. theories on investments. This book is here to help you talk to *each other* about the money you are earning as a team these days. Even if you keep separate finances, you still need to talk about how you want to divvy up the responsibilities around the place, so don't fool yourself into thinking it means you don't have to talk about how to manage these difficult subjects!

- **WHERE CAN I GET ADDITIONAL INFORMATION IF I WANT IT?** At the end of some sections, and within some sections, there are references and tips about books that I have found helpful through the years in taking a realistic look at my finances with my partner.

- **WHEN SHOULD WE USE THIS BOOK?** This book can be used as soon as the decision is made that you want to be a couple, and finances will be part of that union in some form or another. Some people wait until the honeymoon dust settles. But try not to fall into thinking that once you start working on things like household finances that the honeymoon is over. It can be a fun joint project, and something only the two of you share. It's especially fun when you reach those tough financial goals. For example, no one else will know you are secretly sharing for that condo in Bermuda!

- **HOW SHOULD THIS BOOK BE USED?** Use this book as a guidance document and a moderator to keep financial topics focused on the issue at the table. The questions try to hit the major bumps in the road, but if you have others, discuss those couple-specific topics as well. You should probably touch on all the chapters, but if there are certain topics that are more sensitive than others, spend your time as a couple on that subject. Add your own thoughts. There is plenty of extra space at the end of each section throughout the book for notes and specific ideas about your own financial relationship. Give each other homework assignments, and ask the risky financial questions during that safe time set aside when using this book and specifically talking about your finances as a couple. Don't bring up the risky questions at the Thanksgiving table.

- **WHY SHOULD I USE THIS BOOK?** Whether we like it or not, money is important to all of us. Whether we have a lot or a little, we need to manage the money in the best way we as a couple are able to do this and reach our financial goals—whatever they may be. Whether we are in the black or the red, we all have financial goals that can be reached if everyone on the team knows (and agrees on) what the goals of saving the money are.
Money affects all of us. If you don't talk about how you both want to manage your money, you'll both think that you want to manage money the same way. Communication avoids that moment when one of you thinks you have been saving for a condo in Bermuda, and the other thinks you've been saving for a major contribution to your local charitable organization.
This book should be used as the moderator to get important financial questions out in the open and discussed. Answers may not always come on the first round of discussions, but don't despair! You have a lifetime to figure out the answers that best suit you as a couple.

THE EXECUTIVE SUMMARY

Always remember your C-A-S-H.

C — Communicate your financial past with your partner. Consider that you are both coming from different financial histories. You need to explain your financial past to each other. You have a financial past well before you ever earned a dime. Think about it for a minute. Explain to each other how your parents handled money, how it has generally been expected that you handle money, or even if you have never been given the responsibility to handle money. Not having a past where you were responsible for your money equals a type of past with money that your partner should understand. It doesn't mean you lack understanding of financial matters, it just means you need to learn financial management with your partnership from scratch. We all come from a family financial model that we either want to model our own finances after—or run fast and far from. Always consider that in addition to your thoughts, goals, fears and dreams for money spending, saving and management, you have your partner's many thoughts, goals, fears and dreams to seriously consider now, too.

A — Assess where your finances are right now. You have become a couple. So, assess on a routine basis how you are managing the money now in the present. Are the finances the way you as a couple have planned them? Do you need to change your spending habits or your saving habits? Re-allocating finances six months after you have set up a financial plan doesn't spell failure, it spells understanding from both of you in the couple that you have thought about your finances and now it's time for a change.

S — Share your thoughts on future changes to your financial planning with each other. Set aside time to discuss these changes. Your future as a couple will hold many changes you cannot possibly imagine now—many of them financial changes, or life changes based on non-voluntary changes in financial standing. Share your changing thoughts with your partner often. If the topic of financial management is a tough one to bring up, set a meeting date with your partner. It's up to you both to make money a topic you don't have to dread and fight about. If that is not enough incentive, set up a reward for after your financial meeting is over. My favorite reward after a tough financial topic is always a great dinner at the favorite restaurant of the moment.

H — Hear what your partner is telling you when discussing past, present and future financial management goals for your partnership. Respect what your partner is communicating to you about their financial goals. You and your partner both will have many solutions for each financial problem you run into in your relationship. Assess the problem and list the solutions. Sometimes, your solution as a team will end up more successful than any single solution either of you could have come up with as an individual.

I. Pre-Nuptial Agreements and the Wedding Plans

Discussion:

Pre-nuptial agreements:

Pre-nuptial agreements have been in existence for a long time. They help to review finances prior to becoming a couple, and decide what can be shared and what cannot be shared. It also helps when assessing how division will occur if the relationship dissolves. This book only covers a couple of discussion topics related to these pre-nuptial agreements.

However, this book does look at the fun side of contracts within a couple's financial planning, and how a contract signed by both people in the partnership toward a mutual goal may help to keep the couple focused on achieving that financial goal.

It is important that if you do decide to enter into a prenuptial agreement, it is for all the right reasons. Make sure power over the spouse is not the reason. Seriously, make sure you don't just like having more money or jewels or whatever you have. Make sure inevitable divorce or splitting up is not the reason. Make sure secrecy and a hidden life like in the movies is not the reason. But I digress; I just stress that you make sure that you enter into the prenuptial agreement for the right reasons. Marriage isn't about secrets from each other, it's about strength in numbers—specifically the two of you.

My other thought on different financial agreements or contracts between partners is this. As I said in the beginning of this section, financial contracts do not have to be burdens. My husband and I make financial agreements and contracts all the time. It's part of the negotiation process of getting everything we want financially out of our lives. These are great for both of us. For example, if we strive to pay off the mortgage early (my goal), we also still commit to at least one vacation per year (his goal).

If you don't feel the need for any official agreement, try some fun "contracts" with each other. They can be a secret in the partnership, bonding you both, and making the financial goal fun.

Wedding plans:

And, while on the topic of pre-wedding financial plans, if you have this book early enough in your relationship, you may want to make sure you have discussed the financial implications of the Big Day. Remember, some want to elope and pick up dinner on the road, while others want a wedding day that costs more than your car. Sometimes the romantic in the relationship is the bride, sometimes it's the groom, and sometimes it's just one of those things that snowballs out of control until you are in such a state of confusion you have nothing you originally wanted.

So, what should you do about this mass confusion? Together, as a team, make sure your Big Day is just that. You two need to come to a decision about what sort of a day you both want for your wedding. Ensuring that you are not outside of your budget on wedding plans helps you both to be relaxed during the day and not worrying about anything other than the special occasion that it is. Sit down for just a few minutes and plan what you both see as the perfect day, both physically and financially, before you talk to others about their advice. Are you on the same page? Or are you in different books altogether?

In addition to being complicated affairs with emotional decisions regarding family, friends, religion, location and honeymoon spot, there is also the all-important issue of who is paying for everything, and to what extent are you willing to go into debt over the Big Day. You will both need to know if you are paying for this wedding on your own, or if parents or other family will want to help with the wedding bills. The two of you should also decide whether or not you want to make this a simple affair, put it on the credit card, or take out a loan. None of these financial answers are the wrong answer, as long as you can both commit to the final decision and live with any implications the decision holds. For example, can you live with the fact that the day isn't the wedding day you always dreamed it would be because you skimped on the wedding dress? Or, can you live with the fact that you will be paying for this 24-hour period for the next two years instead of saving for your first home?

BRIDE

To Do:
Pre-Nuptial Agreements
1) Discuss how you feel about pre-nuptial agreements with each other. Many times, these can be emotional documents. What do these documents mean to you? Are they important to you, and if they are, seriously ask yourself why. Is it that you have trust issues with your partner? Or is it just that you want to make sure that Great Aunt Ethel gets taken care of no matter what happens to you as a couple.
2) Discuss other types of contracts that you may want to draft with each other. Are there long-term goals that you would like to reach as a couple? If so, are you willing to give up something else in return for that goal?

Wedding Plans
1) Seriously, how much do you want to spend on the wedding day?
2) How willing are you to go into debt for the wedding day?
    a) How will you pay this debt?
    b) Over what time period are you willing to pay the debt off?
    c) Will you both contribute equally to paying off this debt?
3) What are the basic financial thoughts about your wedding:
    a) price for each other's wedding rings
    b) number of guests
    c) location of the wedding
    d) location of the reception
    e) photographer
    f) time of day, type of food
    g) flowers
    h) important bills
       - gifts for the guests
       - gifts for the attendants
    i) honeymoon
    j) other

Make an itemized chart with for this information with an estimate for each. Update it as you obtain actual amounts. Make sure you both agree on the "Maximum" column amounts before you spend that much, or, worse yet, exceed it!

Item	Estimate	Maximum	Actual 1	Actual 2
Invitations				
Wedding dress				
Wedding rings				
Number of guests				
Wedding location				
Reception location				
Photographer				
Meal type				
Flowers (house, wedding location, reception)				
Guest gifts				
Attendant gifts				
Honeymoon				
Thank you notes				

GROOM

To Do:
Pre-Nuptial Agreements
1) Discuss how you feel about pre-nuptial agreements with each other. Many times, these can be emotional documents. What do these documents mean to you? Are they important to you, and if they are, seriously ask yourself why. Is it that you have trust issues with your partner? Or is it just that you want to make sure that Great Aunt Ethel gets taken care of no matter what happens to you as a couple.
2) Discuss other types of contracts that you may want to draft with each other. Are there long-term goals that you would like to reach as a couple? If so, are you willing to give up something else in return for that goal?

Wedding Plans
1) Seriously, how much do you want to spend on the wedding day?
2) How willing are you to go into debt for the wedding day?
   a) How will you pay this debt?
   b) Over what time period are you willing to pay the debt off?
   c) Will you both contribute equally to paying off this debt?
3) What are the basic financial thoughts about your wedding:
   a) price for each other's wedding rings
   b) number of guests
   c) location of the wedding
   d) location of the reception
   e) photographer
   f) time of day, type of food
   g) flowers
   h) important bills
     - gifts for the guests
     - gifts for the attendants
   i) honeymoon
   j) other

Make an itemized chart with for the above information with an estimate for each. Update it as you obtain actual amounts. Make sure you both agree on the "Maximum" column amounts before you spend that much, or, worse yet, exceed it!

Item	Estimate	Maximum	Actual 1	Actual 2
Invitations				
Wedding dress				
Wedding rings				
Number of guests				
Wedding location				
Reception location				
Photographer				
Meal type				
Flowers (house, wedding location, reception)				
Guest gifts				
Attendant gifts				
Honeymoon				
Thank you notes				

II. Sharing

Discussion:

It is true that this book focuses on the couple that plans on consolidating their gains as well as their losses. Remember, money comes in a lot of different forms. Although you may want to share the majority of your finances, there may be a few pieces of your past that you are not willing to dissolve into a partnership, or share at this point in the relationship.

It doesn't mean that the marriage is doomed if you do not want to share everything coming out of the chute. It means you are honest. So, at some point in the beginning of the relationship, the two of you will need to tally up your list of debts and credits, and decide what becomes a part of this great partnership, and what stays with the individual. Try to be reasonable about your sharing. Look honestly at where your debts and credits fall.

Keeping a debt may be as important to one spouse as sharing a similar debt is to the other spouse. Communicating why you want to share certain parts of your financial past when you get married and why you don't want to share other parts of your financial past helps to keep the two of you understanding each other's final goals in your marriage.

Communicating why you want to not share certain credits into the marriage is also important. Give yourself the time you need to figure out why you are not able to share that certain account with your spouse. Then, when you take the time to honestly tell your spouse why you don't want to share some of the money, this conversation will be calm and flowing, not angry and defensive. For example, would your husband really be upset with you if you told him you wanted to keep your college savings account from your six years as a waitress because you really feel like that money is sweat and tears now deserving of cashmere and spa trips? And would your wife be upset if you kept the cash you saved from all those Christmas cards your uncle gave you all those years?

BRIDE

To Do:

Sharing finances provokes strong emotional and defensive feelings. Don't be surprised when yours are stirred. They are supposed to be, or you are not taking this exercise seriously. When the real questions occur, you should not be surprised at how you truly react. Your partner should not feel frustrated that your reactions are entirely different than those you put forward when working in this book. Many people are willing to share their lives, but not so much their money. So take the time to review these questions together as a team. Write down your answers and be specific so there is no misunderstanding when you jump from topic to topic. For example, when you both say it's fine to share credit cards—do you mean all credit cards and the debt collected on all cards to date? Are there limits to new individual debts that you incur? (Or is every sale an invitation not to be passed up?)

1) Do you plan on joining ALL accounts?
2) Do you plan on joining some accounts and leaving others for independent use (and payment)? Discuss why you choose not to join the remaining accounts.
3) If only one partner works outside the home, how will money be allocated?
4) Checkbooks—Do you plan on having a joint checking account? Will you balance it together on a monthly basis? Will you take turns balancing the account?
5) How will bills be paid? Will they be paid monthly together? Will you take turns paying out the bills? Will you take responsibility for separate bills?
6) If you have separate accounts, how will you address problems if the other is behind on payments? How would you like to be helped if your payments fall behind?
7) If there is a difference in earnings, will the partner with the higher income be responsible for more of the joint debt? Will all the communal expenses be shared equally? Will each person have some independent spending money each month that they can spend as they wish? Will each contribute to a joint savings account?
8) What will you do with your tax return refund?
9) How will you decide what to do if you have different opinions? Can you even say compromise? Mediate?

GROOM

To Do:

Sharing finances provokes strong emotional and defensive feelings. Don't be surprised when yours are stirred. They are supposed to be, or you are not taking this exercise seriously. When the real questions occur, you should not be surprised at how you truly react. Your partner should not feel frustrated that your reactions are entirely different than those you put forward when working in this book. Many people are willing to share their lives, but not so much their money. So take the time to review these questions together as a team. Write down your answers and be specific so there is no misunderstanding when you jump from topic to topic. For example, when you both say it's fine to share credit cards—do you mean all credit cards and the debt collected on all cards to date? Are there limits to new individual debts that you incur? (Or is every game ticket an invitation not to be passed up?)

1) Do you plan on joining ALL accounts?
2) Do you plan on joining some accounts and leaving others for independent use (and payment)? Discuss why you choose not to join the remaining accounts.
3) If only one partner works outside the home, how will money be allocated?
4) Checkbooks—Do you plan on having a joint checking account? Will you balance it together on a monthly basis? Will you take turns balancing the account?
5) How will bills be paid? Will they be paid monthly together? Will you take turns paying out the bills? Will you take responsibility for separate bills?
6) If you have separate accounts, how will you address problems if the other is behind on payments? How would you like to be helped if your payments fall behind?
7) If there is a difference in earnings, will the partner with the higher income be responsible for more of the joint debt? Will all the communal expenses be shared equally? Will each person have some independent spending money each month that they can spend as they wish? Will each contribute to a joint savings account?
8) What will you do with your tax return refund?
9) How will you decide what to do if you have different opinions? Can you even say compromise? Mediate?

Brainstorm together and use the itemized chart below to begin to draft the different accounts you both currently use. Remember, this is not the full inventory, but more of an exercise to help you realize all that you both have and how you want to share it. You can then decide together if these accounts should be shared, separate, or cancelled.

Accounts	Bride	Groom
Credit Card		
Debit Card		
Savings Account		
Checking Account		
School Loan		
Paycheck		
Other incomes		
Tax Refund / Bill		
Car loan		

III. Budgets

Discussion:

Budgets are hard. But a budget does not have to be this looming spreadsheet that you can never keep in balance. Instead, you and your partner can see a budget as a simple tracking plan. For the first few months, or years, of your partnership, track how you spend your money. Did you think it was all going to the house, but really it's all going to the cars? These are the types of questions you can answer.

For example, when I was first married, there was a certain amount of disposable income I could not track down. It turns out, it was all going to our Friday night dinners, movies and other date night fun. Learning this quickly helped me to accept the fact that I could sometimes work an entire day to support my weekend plans. Once this was accepted as fact, it made the tracking system seem more stable and realistic, and I enjoyed my dinner out feeling like I had really earned it. (Of course, there were times that eating out had to take a back seat to paying the oil bill.)

Your budget or tracking system can include a few simple subject headings like:

a) credit cards,
b) electricity,
c) phone bills,
d) vacation account,
e) cable/television,
f) any regular monthly expense that you and your spouse have—include ticket costs if they are on a regular basis.

As you go through the first year in your marriage, certain bills will become routine, monthly bills specific to your marriage, and you can add these to your budget or tracking system. There are many books out there telling you that having a budget will solve all of your problems. It won't. So, try a simpler method first. Set up a spreadsheet for the purposes of *tracking your expenses*. Make sure the spreadsheet setup works for you as a couple, and that you are both comfortable using it. It won't work if neither of you ever puts the numbers in the chart! Track your spending for a few months without changing your spending habits, unless of course, you are already in debt.

After you have tracked your spending as a couple, and know where your paychecks are going, *then* set limits according to what you know you can practically spend, and what you can really afford. If you are saving for something big, leave room in the budget for what you've saved, so you both feel good about what finances you are tracking each month together. Congratulate yourselves as a couple for committing to saving for something great or getting out of debt as a family. Remember to set up a practical range for your spending, including the box for the big ticket items and the unforeseen monthly emergency circumstances that always happen. To this day, our family uses a tracking system, not a budgeting system, to take the mystery out of any unusual money disappearances.

BRIDE

To Do:

Sit down with your spouse at the computer, in front of a ledger, or like I do, in front of a huge piece of poster board paper. Answer these three basic questions below before you set up your budget, or tracking system. Then, mark out the sections, and start planning for your future financial goals by tracking your current spending together.

1) Do you believe in budgeting all of your finances, or will tracking your finances be enough for you both?
2) What are the basics you both need in your budget?
3) Do you believe a budget should have a "Fun" account? According to your current finances, how much could be spent in that account before you should start to worry?

Remember, you should really consider tracking your finances first without the stress of limits over your head. This exercise is usually more fun if you set up your tracking system before you are in debt. If you are in debt, it's a great idea to focus part of your tracking system on repaying loans or credit cards. This exercise is also more rewarding if you don't set up your system for failure. Don't include unnecessary monthly payments that will put you into debt after a year.

This should be a bonding exercise for you both, not an ulcer producing exercise that neither of you follows through on because it's just too stressful to remind yourself you are in debt every month. Make sure you aren't setting goals before you even know where your starting line is.

GROOM

To Do:

Sit down with your spouse at the computer, in front of a ledger, or like I do, in front of a huge piece of poster board paper. Answer these three basic questions below before you set up your budget, or tracking system. Then, mark out the sections, and start planning for your future financial goals by tracking your current spending together.

1) Do you believe in budgeting all of your finances, or will tracking your finances be enough for you both?
2) What are the basics you both need in your budget?
3) Do you believe a budget should have a "Fun" account? According to your current finances, how much could be spent in that account before you should start to worry?

Remember, you should really consider tracking your finances first without the stress of limits over your head. This exercise is usually more fun if you set up your tracking system before you are in debt. If you are in debt, it's a great idea to focus part of your tracking system on repaying loans or credit cards. This exercise is also more rewarding if you don't set up your system for failure. Don't include unnecessary monthly payments that will put you into debt after a year.

This should be a bonding exercise for you both, not an ulcer producing exercise that neither of you follows through on because it's just too stressful to remind yourself you are in debt every month. Make sure you aren't setting goals before you even know where your starting line is.

IV. Debt and Surplus

Discussion:

Some of us need to be in the black. Some of us can excuse a car payment and a mortgage, but all else must be paid off. Some of us don't think about our debt to income ratio until the car gets repossessed. This goes back to the "C" of always thinking about your **C-A-S-H**. We all have to consider where we came from with our financial histories. Some of us grew up needing constant financial security; some of us grew up without two nickels in the bank. You each have to be sensitive to these issues when you work with your partner to create a financial future for you both. You need to consider where you came from and how comfortable you are with your current financial situation and how you want to join your finances with your partner's.

In addition, many people will have different definitions of debt and surplus. Recent graduates may tell you that as long as they can pay their minimum balance on the credit card every month, they are not in debt. Any conservative will tell you unless you have cash saved in the bank for bills to be paid months ahead, you are doomed to being in debt forever. Make sure you and your spouse agree on your definitions of debt and surplus.

I cannot stress enough in this book that even if you choose not to join finances, it does not mean that you can avoid knowing and understanding your partner's financial portfolio. You are still a partnership that needs to work together toward the same goals. Knowing each other's financial standing and where your comfort level is with debt and surplus is important in setting realistic goals for you both.

BRIDE

To Do:
1) How comfortable are you when you are "in the red"? Are you normally in debt? If so, how much debt do you carry every month?
2) If you have money, do you need to spend it immediately? Or can you see the distant future and save for it?
3) Do you always carry money with you? If so, how much?
4) How much do you spend on "extras" in a week? How much does your partner spend on "extras" per week?
5) What are these extras? Lunches? Coffees? Magazines? Entertainment after work? Spa trips?

On the conservative side, many financial planners will tell you that you should always have approximately six months net salary saved in the bank above and beyond your normal operating expenses to cover any unforeseen circumstances. These unforeseen circumstances might include situations such as the sudden loss of a job, emergency need for a new vehicle, a sick pet, or a new furnace. That said, do either of you have a financial history that would have you fall onto the conservative side? You and your partner should talk about this saving strategy. Then, assess how much six months net salary is for you both, and if you both believe you need this much.

If you believe you would need more to get by, you should decide if this is because your spending habits are uncontrolled beyond your earnings, or because you are ultraconservative. Then, you should share this with your spouse. Uncontrollable conservatives have a long list of potential unforeseen circumstances to consider and can estimate years of net salaries will be needed to provide for the hidden expenses. For those of you that are less cautious with your long term savings, you should consider sharing where you want to be with your partner in ten years, and if never saving long term could still get you there.

GROOM

To Do:

1) How comfortable are you when you are "in the red"? Are you normally in debt? If so, how much debt do you carry every month?

2) If you have money, do you need to spend it immediately? Or can you see the distant future and save for it?

3) Do you always carry money with you? If so, how much?

4) How much do you spend on "extras" in a week? How much does your partner spend on "extras" per week?

5) What are these extras? Lunches? Coffees? Magazines? Entertainment after work? Ski trips?

On the conservative side, many financial planners will tell you that you should always have approximately six months net salary saved in the bank above and beyond your normal operating expenses to cover any unforeseen circumstances. These unforeseen circumstances might include situations such as the sudden loss of a job, emergency need for a new vehicle, a sick pet, or a new furnace. That said, do either of you have a financial history that would have you fall onto the conservative side? You and your partner should talk about this saving strategy. Then, assess how much six months net salary is for you both, and if you both believe you need this much.

If you believe you would need more to get by, you should decide if this is because your spending habits are uncontrolled beyond your earnings, or because you are ultra conservative. Then, you should share this with your spouse. Uncontrollable conservatives have a long list of potential unforeseen circumstances to consider and can estimate years of net salaries will be needed to provide for the hidden expenses. For those of you that are less cautious with your long term savings, you should consider sharing where you want to be with your partner in ten years, and if never saving long term could still get you there.

V. Credit Cards

This topic follows well on the heels of the debt and surplus subject. Understanding credit cards and the debt (as well as frequent flier miles and free shipping perks) that can rapidly ensue are important to each of us once we become independent. The importance is greater once we form a partnership. Credit cards can also be an amazing and simple way to keep your finances organized and in one place. With these cards you can track and understand your spending faster than any ATM machine could ever spit out cash receipts.

You should at this point know each other's credit card debt and whether or not you will be sharing each other's debt from these cards. Remember, even if you are not sharing financial responsibilities, you should know where each other stands financially.

Discussion:
How do you each feel about being in debt? Each person has what is called a risk tolerance level. Risk tolerance is applicable for everything from physical activities (chess vs. skydiving) to finance (bank accounts vs. stock market). It is important for each of you to understand, if not necessarily agree, where your partner stands with this risk tolerance. It is unfair of you to ask your partner to invest heavily in the stock market if your partner is highly risk averse. The partner will be constantly nervous and agitated about the investment. Maybe you cannot agree with that level of safety, but you must understand it for your partner's sake. Ask each other questions to find out how each of you feels about money spending. Specifically, how do each of you feel about being in debt with credit cards? What is the level of debt with which each of you are comfortable? What is the level of debt that is unacceptable to you? You know the level that makes you uneasy, keeps you awake at night worrying about which bills you won't be able to pay, or makes you feel downright annoyed with your partner for thinking you could ever manage money in such a way.

Debt is not fun. In fact, money management gets less fun to discuss as you and your spouse get more in debt. Take the bull by the horns, and draw yourself away from the debt. The sooner in the partnership you understand you and your partner's spending habits, the sooner you will control debt.

There are some simple basic definitions that you, as a responsible credit card holder, should know about a credit card:
<u>Annual Fees:</u> Simply stated, this is the yearly payment you must make to the credit card company for the privilege of using their credit card.
Note: Many cards that have an annual fee offer money back at the end of the year, or free miles on airlines or other benefits if you carry their credit card. Be warned. Many

times these benefits require huge amounts of spending before they pay off into great dreams of flights to Hawaii.

You must pay this annual fee before you can start to acquire the benefits of the credit card. Make sure your benefits that you will earn with your credit card aren't washed out with the high annual fee you have to pay.

If you don't get any benefits with your credit card, but there is an annual fee, you may want to consider changing to a credit card that doesn't charge an annual fee. There are so many credit card companies out there, and they all want your business. So, be choosy about your credit card. Try to make sure it's the right fit for your spending habits.

If all of your credit cards have interest rates at seventeen percent, and your partner's rate is eleven percent, it's important to see that financially, your spouse's credit cards are the way to go if and when you begin consolidating. If he has had bad customer service experience with his card, but you have received several extensions for bill paying on your card, that's also something to consider.

I have a credit card only in my name because the company offers free shipping on their products. My spouse has an allegiance to the local childhood bank account, so we have a joint account there. Pick your battles carefully. These little oddities won't make or break the financial model you have set up. But, there are major points that you both need to address when it comes to sharing.

Annual Percentage Rate (APR): Again, to simplify, this is the percentage rate that is applied to the balance on your monthly billing statement every month if you don't pay the bill the month it is due. So, you are paying interest on any amount in your bill that you don't pay off each month. This means that if you don't pay a bill in January, your February statement will add interest from your January statement. In February, you will pay interest on the interest that was accrued in January. This interest rate is not nominal. In some cases, the percentage rate of a credit card can reach over twenty per cent if circumstances are poor with past credit.

Some notes to remember on percentage rates and potential downfalls with a credit card.

You should check out the small print on your credit card when it comes to cash advances. No one is saying it isn't handy to have the option of being able to get cash advances from your credit card, but sometimes the interest rate can be staggering on these advances. This is a great idea to have the cash advance on your credit card for any emergency, just be smart as a couple about how you use your cards.

Also, check out the fine print when it comes to late payments and percentage rates related to late payments on your credit cards. Under most credit card contracts, you must pay a late payment to the company each time your payment is sent late. In addition, some credit card contracts will default to higher annual percentage rates if your account extends beyond the due date.

Note: When a credit card company tries to lure you away from your current card by telling you to transfer your balance to a much lower percentage rate, you should know that it is possible that credit card companies may be manipulating your money. Sometimes, it's only the transferred balance that is getting the lower percentage rate, not any new purchases that you may be putting on your card. The company may then let you pay these low interest rate balances first, while your high interest rate payments are piling up. So, here you are thinking you're getting rid of your old debt, but now your new purchases are racking up a huge new debt on a huge new percentage rate for you. Not good.

You should know all of these facts about your credit card and be able to manage your debt on the card at all times. Your partner should know if you have ever not been able to manage the debt that accrued on your credit card, and how (if at all) you were able to come out of that situation. You each need to know the other's financial strengths and weaknesses.

Every company in existence wants to sell you a credit card. Why? Because that credit card APR rate is so much higher than any bank loan rate, that once your credit card debt gets too high for you to manage, you will forever on just be paying that credit card company their interest rate. You will never get out of the credit hole. Remember, you should look to find the best finance rates on credit cards, and try not to put your debt into credit cards. Credit cards, although simple to use, have very high interest rates. Beware.

BRIDE

To Do:

Following are some questions on credit card basics that you should know about each other's credit card history. Go through these questions together. These are team questions which, based on each of your financial histories, may have a lot of "Why would we do that?" questions to follow. Make sure to discuss all of this with each other. Remember, this is not just a book to get through to pass a course; this is a book to make your partnership run smoother. When finances run smoothly, you can focus on the rest of your partnership together. Answer these questions seriously and take each other's concerns about debt and credit use to heart. Communicating these concerns now will stop a lot of unnecessary frustration down the line.

1) Do you know how much debt each person has in credit today?
2) Are you the type of person that must pay off credit bills each month and never have a balance?
3) Do you know what your goal is as a partnership to bring this debt to in the next year?
4) Do you both have credit cards?
5) Will you keep the credit cards in your own names?
6) Will you each put each other on your credit cards?
7) Will you drop the higher interest credit card and consolidate on one mutual credit card?
8) Will you close out certain cards and start fresh with a new account for both partners?
9) How do you feel about having a balance on a credit card? Is it just part of the monthly bill? Do you have to pay it off or else you feel uncomfortable?

GROOM

To Do:

Following are some questions on credit card basics that you should know about each other's credit card history. Go through these questions together. These are team questions which, based on each of your financial histories, may have a lot of "Why would we do that?" questions to follow. Make sure to discuss all of this with each other. Remember, this is not just a book to get through to pass a course; this is a book to make your partnership run smoother. When finances run smoothly, you can focus on the rest of your partnership together. Answer these questions seriously and take each other's concerns about debt and credit use to heart. Communicating these concerns now will stop a lot of unnecessary frustration down the line.

1) Do you know how much debt each person has in credit today?
2) Are you the type of person that must pay off credit bills each month and never have a balance?
3) Do you know what your goal is as a partnership to bring this debt to in the next year?
4) Do you both have credit cards?
5) Will you keep the credit cards in your own names?
6) Will you each put each other on your credit cards?
7) Will you drop the higher interest credit card and consolidate on one mutual credit card?
8) Will you close out certain cards and start fresh with a new account for both partners?
9) How do you feel about having a balance on a credit card? Is it just part of the monthly bill? Do you have to pay it off or else you feel uncomfortable?

VI. Professional Careers

Discussion:

Almost all of us feel some sense of satisfaction when we have a job, a career, and a place to go that needs our professional work product. Some feel this sense of satisfaction a bit more strongly than others. Some even define themselves by their jobs. If you ask them what they "do", they will tell you they are engineers or teachers, not that they love to play the piano or hike every weekend. This section of the book looks at exactly how each of you feel about your jobs, and how tied you are to making sure you have a career to talk about at the cocktail party on Friday night.

Professional careers pave the way to talking about your financial status as a couple. If you are satisfied in your career, you will most likely stay in your current profession, excel at what you do, and usually become very financially stable over time.

On the other hand, if you are not tied to your profession or feel loyal to the position at your company emotionally, you may be constantly switching jobs, changing salary grades, perhaps even moving frequently to where the job site is located. You may even have hopes of discontinuing your career after you are married.

These feelings you both have about your professional careers are important to share. One of you may not be able to handle the instability of never knowing where the next paycheck will come from. If that's so, the other person should realize that in order to have financial stability, they will always have to work. On the other hand, one of you may be dedicated enough to travel around the world in order to see each project in your career to a successful end. In this case, it is important for the spouse to know that the family may have to be transported whenever the new project starts.

BRIDE

To Do:

In this section, it is important to first review these questions by yourself, before coming into the conversation with your partner. This is because you want to make sure you are being true to your own long term goals. If you honestly feel you will always need to have some type of career outside the family to fulfill your needs, make sure you communicate this to your partner. If you honestly feel there are millions of different volunteer duties and stay at home responsibilities that could keep you occupied until the cows come home, this should be known as well. And, let us not forget, if there are those out there who hate their current positions in the grind as they know it, and cannot wait until the days of nine to five are over, this needs to be communicated as well. The choice of wanting part-time and exploring other opportunities that are out there, but only being able to do this with the help of a supportive spouse, needs to be communicated as well.

1) Are you happy at your current job?
   a. Do you see yourself there in that position or a similar position and happy about it for a period of time?
   b. If you could quit this job, would you?
   c. What would you do instead?
2) If you were offered a job in a different area of the country, or world for that matter, would you consider moving for the sake of your career?
   a. Would you move for your spouse's career and find something new for yourself once you had moved there?
3) To what degree would salary play a part in your decision to uproot to another part of the country?
   a. What would your salary need to be to move to a different area?
   b. If children were involved, what would the salary need to be?
4) How frustrating would your job need to be before you would walk away from your job and the salary it affords you?
5) Do you see yourself in your job for a period of time and earning a steady income?
   a. Do you see your job as something to get you by until something better comes along?
6) Do you plan on working once you are a couple?
7) Is it important for you to advance beyond your current position?
   a. Is this because you would like to advance to more responsibility, or because you would like to earn a higher salary? Or a bit of both?

GROOM

To Do:
In this section, it is important to first review these questions by yourself, before coming into the conversation with your partner. This is because you want to make sure you are being true to your own long term goals. If you honestly feel you will always need to have some type of career outside the family to fulfill your needs, make sure you communicate this to your partner. If you honestly feel there are millions of different volunteer duties and stay at home responsibilities that could keep you occupied until the cows come home, this should be known as well. And, let us not forget, if there are those out there who hate their current positions in the grind as they know it, and cannot wait until the days of nine to five are over, this needs to be communicated as well. The choice of wanting part-time and exploring other opportunities that are out there, but only being able to do this with the help of a supportive spouse, needs to be communicated as well.

1) Are you happy at your current job?
   a. Do you see yourself there in that position or a similar position and happy about it for a period of time?
   b. If you could quit this job, would you?
   c. What would you do instead?
2) If you were offered a job in a different area of the country, or world for that matter, would you consider moving for the sake of your career?
   a. Would you move for your spouse's career and find something new for yourself once you had moved there?
3) To what degree would salary play a part in your decision to uproot to another part of the country?
   a. What would your salary need to be to move to a different area?
   b. If children were involved, what would the salary need to be?
4) How frustrating would your job need to be before you would walk away from your job and the salary it affords you?
5) Do you see yourself in your job for a period of time and earning a steady income?
   a. Do you see your job as something to get you by until something better comes along?
6) Do you plan on working once you are a couple?
7) Is it important for you to advance beyond your current position?
   a. Is this because you would like to advance to more responsibility, or because you would like to earn a higher salary? Or a bit of both?

VII. Investments

Discussion:

This chapter again deals with the phrase <u>Risk Tolerance</u>. If both you and your partner had the exact same risk tolerance, you would have very little to disagree about when it came to investing. It is really rare when two people agree down to the last penny where the money should be invested. So, take the time to understand why your spouse refuses to invest in the stock you think you both can retire on. Remember that expression: C-A-S-H. It will help to ease tension and help you both to better manage your joint accounts. Here are some definitions to remember when talking investing with your spouse.

<u>Risk Averse:</u> You do not like to take risks with your money. Keeping up with inflation suits you just fine. Investing in the stock market is not a stable enough investment for you.

<u>Risk Tolerant:</u> You take risks with your money. The payouts may be fewer but they are much larger.

<u>Diversified Portfolio:</u> A portfolio with a little bit investment for the risk averse, and a little bit for the risk tolerant. When a couple develops a diversified portfolio, they are almost always certain to have investments that will please both the risk tolerant and the risk averse. If you are both risk tolerant or risk averse, you may consider bringing in a financial advisor, someone who can help both of you see the benefits of investing in a different way than you currently are managing your money.

You must again realize that as a couple, for all of your similarities, you will have differences in your level of risk when investing. Try to place yourself on a scale of 1—5 for how risk averse you are (one being the lowest, and five the highest). It is imperative that you and your partner understand this level of risk and invest accordingly.

Remember also that there are financial advisors out there of all different types. Some advisors, if they have the type of personality that works with the two of you, can be very helpful in being a moderator between the two of you if you just cannot agree on your financial investments. A third person is not a weakness. Instead, that person is an objective financial ear to listen to the couple's two theories on investments and help negotiate a settlement you will both be comfortable with. But be warned, you should definitely check out your advisor and ask for references or background and ensure the person is truly objective. It can be a difficult process to find the right advisor for you as a couple, but once you have one, that person may be a lifesaver as you grow in your financial relationship.

Web Sites:

If you would like to look at different sources of financial information on saving, spending and investment issues on a web site before you both talk to a third party, there are many helpful web sites out there. I have listed only a few below that I have used in the past. A simple web search can bring many other interesting and fun sites to your attention. On a rainy Saturday, it may be interesting to log on and see what tips you can find and agree on together for financial strategies for your money.

www.bankofamerica.com This is a great web site for using their calculators to find out mortgages, loans, retirement, college savings plans and investment topics. Who can resist a calculator when you get to pick your own interest rate?

www.statefarm.com This is a fun web site to look at car purchasing through. You can calculate both your monthly cost if you lease or buy your car. They also have a section for budgeting. It includes quick budgets for "How much does it cost to raise a child?", "How much am I spending?" and "Should my spouse work, too?" All good topics for discussion, I think!

www.federalreserve.gov This web site is loaded with financial information for a couple to browse through related to personal financial planning. It includes separate sections on consumer credit, car leasing, mortgages, and an entire program on personal finance. Now, it's up to you two, once again, to agree on the personal finance topics that this web site discusses.

BRIDE

To Do:
Before you start writing, take a few minutes to talk with your partner about where you stand when you invest.

Below are some questions for you to discuss to help you become more comfortable about where your groom's investment decisions are coming from based on his financial past, where he wants to invest your money today and why, and where he sees the two of you in ten years financially based on these investment decisions.

Questions:
1) What number did you come up with when you assessed yourself on how risk averse you are? Are your investments historically risk averse or risk tolerant?
2) Do you think about the here-and-now or do you invest for twenty years down the road?
3) Do you enjoy investing in high-risk stocks?
4) Do you want to invest in diversified mutual funds?
5) Is credit union and savings bank a good stable investment to you that matches inflation?
6) Do you already have investments set up? What are the investments? (This is also a good way to tell if you are what you say you are!) How are the investment performance standards compared to the current market? Are you emotionally attached to any of your investments? Will you join your historical investments after you become a partnership?
7) How much do you hope to set aside each month to be invested? Will these investments be joint investments or will you have individual investments without your partner?

GROOM

To Do:

Before you start writing, take a few minutes to talk with your partner about where you stand when you invest.

Here are some questions for you to discuss to help you become more comfortable about where your bride's investment decisions are coming from based on her financial past, where she wants to invest your money today and why, and where she sees the two of you in ten years financially based on these investment decisions.

Questions:

1) What number did you come up with when you assessed yourself on how risk averse you are? Are your investments historically risk averse or risk tolerant?

2) Do you think about the here-and-now or do you invest for twenty years down the road?

3) Do you enjoy investing in high-risk stocks?

4) Do you want to invest in diversified mutual funds?

5) Is credit union and savings bank a good stable investment to you that matches inflation?

6) Do you already have investments set up? What are the investments? (This is also a good way to tell if you are what you say you are!) How are the investment performance standards compared to the current market? Are you emotionally attached to any of your investments? Will you join your historical investments after you become a partnership?

7) How much do you hope to set aside each month to be invested? Will these investments be joint investments or will you have individual investments without your partner?

VIII. Homes

Discussion:

Let's start this chapter off by saying that not everyone wants to own a home. Some want to live in an apartment, pay rent, and never worry about mowing the lawn or shoveling the driveway or raking the leaves. Some work at high stress careers in the city and do not want the horrific commute that living in suburbia would give them, so they choose apartments in the city. We can look at this decision from a financial standpoint as well. Renting, instead of buying, allows for never saving up the initial down payment usually necessary to buy the first home. However, keep in mind that the rent that is paid forever toward the apartment is never put toward owning a final product in the end. You pay for exactly what you use that month, nothing more. You may want to think of your home as an investment option or a place to have when you reach retirement as well as somewhere you live now. This is a topic for discussion with your spouse. Once you both agree on exactly what a home should account for in your financial life, you can decide on whether or not you want a home, and what kind of home you want. This chapter is for the couples who choose to buy a home.

Buying a home is a stressful experience. There is so much more than just figuring out the mortgage rate and locking in. There are competitive rates, and companies who will fight for your business. There are mortgage brokers who will, for a fee, find you the most competitive rates.

You can pay "points" when you initially sign for your mortgage. Simply put, this is money that goes toward interest. Each point equals one percent of your loan amount. You can pay prepaid interest points ahead of time and receive a lower interest rate on the mortgage. This usually happens if you plan on being at the house for a period of time because of the helpful lower interest rate. There is also a second type of points that you pay because you were given a mortgage in the first place.

When you do finally apply for a mortgage, you should know that for the first few years, you will probably end up paying more in interest on your home than principal payments toward the actual purchase price of the home. When you look at your payment coupons for your mortgage, it will show how much interest you pay on your home, and how much principal. It graphs a gradual decrease in interest payments and increase in principal payments over a long period of time that you have agreed to (the life of your mortgage loan). Amortization is a type of payment plan that can be used on debts that have a time schedule for payback, such as your mortgage. Under almost all circumstances, at the start of the loan, you pay a huge amount of interest and a small amount of principal. Later, you pay a huge amount of principal and a small amount of interest. This payment split of interest and principal is found in an amortization table.

These tables can be frustrating in the beginning because of the lack of money that is dedicated to the principal of your mortgage. However, it does get better over time.

Also, keep in mind that you can also put a little extra money into your mortgage coupon payment during the months that you have it and that usually will count toward your principal. Confirm this fact with your mortgage lender, and if that is the case for your mortgage, you may want to consider putting extra money into your mortgage payment each month. Beware of any pre-payment penalties, however. A prepayment penalty is a monetary penalty that is given to homeowners if they pay their mortgage off too soon (before the life of the loan has expired). This type of monthly or annual dedicated spending is a team decision that you should sit down and discuss. If one of you feels strongly about how to pay off the mortgage, discuss that. If you think this type of payment should be assessed on a monthly basis depending on how other bills were in that particular month, you should also be willing to bring it up every month. Every penny counts when it comes to interest and mortgages, and what a great team effort to purchase a house together.

Web Sites:

If you are looking for basic definitions on many of the terms that your bank will be throwing out at you when you apply for a mortgage, you can log on to www.bankofamerica. com. This web site offers very helpful basic information for personal financial planning under a "personal" tab, as well as more technical information as you get deeper into financial projects together, such as undergoing the process of applying for a loan. The web site talks about being a first time home buyer, buying a home, refinancing your home, using home equity, mortgages, and what I have always found helpful, a glossary with a lot of terms in very understandable definitions.

A second very helpful and interesting web site for all of your calculating questions is www.bankrate.com. This web site calculates your car and mortgage monthly payments when you provide the simple information. For homes, simply include the mortgage amount, mortgage term, interest rate of your mortgage and the mortgage start date. The other valuable tool this site provides is an amortization table for your mortgage. It shows you how much, each month, you will be paying toward interest and how much toward principal; the actual payment on the price of your home that you borrowed. This is one of our favorite sites, and we are sure as soon as our principal paid is more than our interest paid each month, we will really enjoy it even more.

A stress free exercise could be to simply sit down together and browse around on these web sites and others mentioned in other sections of this book. Include web sites that you may have been advised about by everyone who insists on giving you this advice. You will find once you both know some of the basics, you will feel more comfortable asking financial questions as they relate to your marriage. As a team, when you go to the banks and the financial advisors and the car dealerships, this will be even more true.

Applying for a mortgage is not an impossible process if you both have a reasonable credit rating. Do not be daunted by your friends and neighbors who insist you will never truly understand all the nuances of buying a home. Everyone is not out to get you during this mortgage application and home buying process. However, you must remember that during this process, no one will be giving away any of their services. You must pay for all of the services you need, and they can add up. Educating yourselves with basic knowledge on the process is your best defense. As a couple, you will both have strengths and using these strengths together can make you a force to be reckoned with.

Talk to each other about the stress you have over the bills that will ultimately add up and need to be paid to everyone before the closing of your home. If you know together how you are each feeling about the enormous responsibility you are taking on, it may seem less gargantuan if you are cranky together. Misery loves company, so be each other's company. And, there is a light at the end of this particular tunnel: your first home together. Plus, you can look together at those positive financial pieces of owning a home and celebrate the small financial victories. For example, all of that interest that you are paying on your home is tax deductible. You can also deduct any of your property taxes that you paid in the past year off the income being taxed. And, since you now have these tax deductions off of your income tax, you may even want to consider adjusting your tax withholdings from your pay check. You could do this because now that you have these additional deductions, your tax burden will be lower, so you can keep more of your money during the year. So, when April 15th comes around, you will have these interest and tax payments to deduct off of the taxes.

You will look knowledgeable and feel more confident as a couple when you start financial discussions with a bank or mortgage lender if you are both educated with the basics of home ownership.

Keep in mind:

Then, there's the whole personal side of buying a home. If you simply want four walls for shelter you are looking for one kind of home. If you are using your home as your major investment as a couple, you are looking for a completely different type of home. There are neighborhoods to consider, towns to consider, school systems (if you so choose) to consider, and so much more. These are the subjects that you need to discuss with your spouse to make sure you both agree on what you want in a home.

You need to consider each other's past personal histories regarding the types of homes you each grew up in as children. Is that type of home and that financial situation something either of you want in your future together? For example, if one of you grew up in a lavish home, but your parents were always arguing because all they could afford was the lavish home, you may conclude that a small affordable home is exactly what your marriage should look for. Communicating the reason why you want this type of home to your spouse is as important as any other part of the home buying process.

BRIDE

To Do:

Answer the following questions honestly to yourself, then come together and answer the questions together. If you don't already own a home, these are important questions to get right. As always, there are no extra points for answering what you think your partner may want to hear.

1) Will the home be bought and deeded in both of your names? If not, how will the buying of the home be completed?

   If it is decided that one person will own the home, and the other pay in the home, how will this be accomplished? And, going back to reasons for answers, why does only one person own the home? Remember, there are many good reasons for having only one person own the home, however, there are many not-so-good reasons as well, power over the partner being one of them. Try to stay away from this.

2) Is it important to you to own a home?

3) What is your comfort level for a mortgage when buying a new home?

4) How much today is practical for you to spend on a home? Remember, this number will change drastically as the years roll on.

5) How much would your luxury home cost—your upper limit to buying a home?

GROOM

To Do:

Answer the following questions honestly to yourself, then come together and answer the questions together. If you don't already own a home, these are important questions to get right. As always, there are no extra points for answering what you think your partner may want to hear.

1) Will the home be bought and deeded in both of your names? If not, how will the buying of the home be completed?

   If it is decided that one person will own the home, and the other pay in the home, how will this be accomplished? And, going back to reasons for answers, why does only one person own the home? Remember, there are many good reasons for having only one person own the home, however, there are many not-so-good reasons as well, power over the partner being one of them. Try to stay away from this.

2) Is it important to you to own a home?

3) What is your comfort level for a mortgage when buying a new home?

4) How much today is practical for you to spend on a home? Remember, this number will change drastically as the years roll on.

5) How much would your luxury home cost—your upper limit to buying a home?

IX. Cars

Discussion:
There are many ways to address owning a car. Some people buy new, some buy used, some people lease. The optimal choice for your partnership is up to you both to decide as a team. Remember that some people see cars as simple modes of transportation, some see them as status symbols. Some use cars as company vehicles believing that the success of their business will be partially judged depending on the car that drives up to the client's home. These are all issues that you used to decide by yourself when you were a single person. You did not have to make the decision of how much you valued the car, or your reasons for the value, with anyone else's input. Now that you are a couple, you must discuss these issues together. You cannot believe that you can separately purchase one car for each of you with individual reasons and never care why your partner made the decision. You should also remember that it is not fair to put a huge car loan on a partner who has concern with debt issues. So just don't. Talk about your car purchase and avoid the famous "buyer's remorse".

When you buy a car but need financing to purchase the car, often times you have the option of either choosing dealer financing with no dealer rebate, or applying for bank financing and taking the dealer rebate. These are choices to talk about so you both know how helpful the rebates really are.

Some insurance companies will send out educational pamphlets to help you make the financial decision between leasing and buying a car. It's a good idea to review these information packages together before heading off to the car dealership. You want to be educated buyers when you walk in to discuss financing with your car dealer who may be offering a rebate. The offer the dealership is making may not always be as beneficial to you as it may seem at first glance. If you prefer the internet, try the web site mentioned in this chapter, as well as other helpful sites you may discover together, that has a calculator for making the decision between leasing and buying your car. It may not seem like a big difference, but if it is only a few dollars every month, why shouldn't the two of you have it to spend on coffee and a walk in the park, as opposed to giving it to your car dealer?

One of the most important points for you as a couple to remember when you are buying a large purchase like your first car is not to feel divided once you enter the dealership. Know what you both need in a car, what you both would like in a car, and what isn't that important for you to have. This will make your bargaining days at the dealership run much more smoothly.

Website:
There are many helpful websites to browse when crunching numbers on everything

car-related including car loan payments, buying your car versus leasing your car, and figuring out how much a loan payment should be by changing the down payment and loan interest rate several times. One web site is www.auto-loan-calculator.bz/index.htm. The web site has a calculator for all the major finance questions you and your spouse will cover when discussing bringing home a new car. I have no doubt that there are nuances to everyone's situation that the web site may or may not cover. However, I also have no doubt that this web site will shed light on finance questions about your car that the two of you may have disagreed on earlier. Be warned, it may not agree with you!

BRIDE

To Do:
Following are a few questions that you can discuss with your spouse.
1) How do you view a car? A luxury item or a practical necessity?
2) How much, at this time in the partnership, would you spend if you bought a car today? Where did you come up with that number?
3) If you had extra money, would you spend it on a car?
4) If you HAD to spend extra money on a car, would you spend it on luxury items on a practical model, or would you move up to the next model level?
5) How many cars do you need in your family?

GROOM

To Do:
Following are a few questions that you can discuss with your spouse.
1) How do you view a car? A luxury item or a practical necessity?
2) How much, at this time in the partnership, would you spend if you bought a car today? Where did you come up with that number?
3) If you had extra money, would you spend it on a car?
4) If you HAD to spend extra money on a car, would you spend it on luxury items on a practical model, or would you move up to the next model level?
5) How many cars do you need in your family?

X. Second Homes and Boats

(and other huge expenses you may or may not be able to afford)

Discussion:

Some time ago, there was a television show called "Lifestyles of the Rich and Famous", which each week profiled the homes and lifestyles of rich and famous people. We would all like a piece of something that someone had on the show. The rustic second home in the Adirondacks, the sail boat, the really great piece of jewelry, the luxurious car, the classic piece of furniture that will be the cornerstone in our new home. What exactly we all want is different, depending on who we are. How badly we each want it is also dependent on who we are. A few things to consider before going overboard and buying everything we want are as follows:

1) Where are we with our credit card debt?
2) Are our investments still making a profit that can afford us a more comfortable lifestyle?
3) Are we risk tolerant enough that we don't mind having extra payments to make on a luxury item in our financial tracking system?
4) If we own a home, where are we with the mortgage payment?
5) How are the car payments coming along?
6) Do we plan on having children?

Take some time as a couple to decide what is really important to you both. If financial security is more important than a boat, make sure your partner, the avid boater, knows that. Make sure you both know what luxury items are worth second loans to each of you in order to afford them. You should always be honest with your comfort level as an individual in purchasing luxury items. Remember, keeping up with the Jones's may fill your competitive spirit, but it may not be healthy for your partnership. Don't hurt your financial relationship with your spouse just so you can brag about the boat you only use twice a year.

BRIDE

To Do:

1) By yourself, make a list of the Ten Most Wanted luxury items *you as an individual* want in the next ten years of your life. You should have fun with this exercise. You're letting your husband know what you see as luxury, and where it fits into your lifestyle.

2) Go head to head with your partner. Each of you now list off *your* Ten Most Wanted list to each other.

3) Negotiate with each other which Top Ten items make the final Top Ten Most Wanted list for *you both as a couple*.

4) Now, with your current salaries, which of these top ten items will you actually try to budget for in your tracking system in the next five years? The next ten years?

LUXURY ITEM	COST	WHEN I WANT IT
1)		
2)		
3)		
4)		
5)		
6)		
7)		
8)		
9)		
10)		

GROOM

To Do:

1) By yourself, make a list of the Ten Most Wanted luxury items *you as an individual* want in the next ten years of your life. You should have fun with this exercise. You're letting your wife know what you see as luxury, and where it fits into your lifestyle.

2) Go head to head with your partner. Each of you now list off *your* Ten Most Wanted list to each other.

3) Negotiate with each other which Top Ten items make the final Top Ten Most Wanted list for *you both as a couple*.

4) Now, with your current salaries, which of these top ten items will you actually try to budget for in your tracking system in the next five years? The next ten years?

LUXURY ITEM	COST	WHEN I WANT IT
1)		
2)		
3)		
4)		
5)		
6)		
7)		
8)		
9)		
10)		

XI. Vacations

Discussion:

Maybe by now the two of you have already taken one or two romantic vacation getaways together. If they were honestly what you were hoping for, then you are all set. You probably don't even need to review this chapter. But it seems to me that how a couple spends on a vacation is always a topic of discussion once they return home. Maybe it's just one partner, sometimes both. Buyer's remorse, some call it, the souvenirs that seemed like a good idea at the time, that lavish dinner out that seemed worth it when compared to the other dinners offered. But, in order for the vacation to be a success, both at the time of the vacation and when the credit card comes for payment, you should discuss your thoughts on payment together. That way, when planning the vacation, you both know how the other feels about splurging on first class airlines, French bistros, and luxury hotel rooms.

BRIDE

To Do:

1) How much per person is a reasonable vacation for you?
   a. Do you want to take different types of vacations at different points in the year? If so, discuss what your February vacation would be like, and your September vacation, etc.
2) How often do you plan to take vacations?
3) Do you enjoy many small vacations, or one luxurious vacation, or do you live for many long luxurious vacations?
4) How do you budget, if at all, for your vacations?
   a. A separate vacation account?
   b. A monthly set-aside?
   c. A withdrawal from savings as needed?
   d. A hit to the credit card?
5) If you plan on children, how will vacations change, if any?
   a. Will you expect more luxury or less?
   b. More vacation time or less time?

GROOM

To Do:

1) How much per person is a reasonable vacation for you?
   a. Do you want to take different types of vacations at different points in the year? If so, discuss what your February vacation would be like, and your September vacation, etc.
2) How often do you plan to take vacations?
3) Do you enjoy many small vacations, or one luxurious vacation, or do you live for many long luxurious vacations?
4) How do you budget, if at all, for your vacations?
   a. A separate vacation account?
   b. A monthly set-aside?
   c. A withdrawal from savings as needed?
   d. A hit to the credit card?
5) If you plan on children, how will vacations change, if any?
   a. Will you expect more luxury or less?
   b. More vacation time or less time?

XII. Retirement and Wills

Discussion:

It seems like so far away, but you need to think about it eventually. You see, if you think about retirement now, and saving now, your money will become more valuable in the future. Now is the time to talk, while you are young and it is not a stressful subject of whether or not you have enough to get you through retirement years. You may only want to discuss retirement in a more general fashion with your partner. You have many years ahead of you before you have to actually retire together, but if you use them wisely, it could make a huge difference in how you live later.

As far as the wills go, find a lawyer and make one out. It may seem morbid, but that's the way it is (especially if you have children, but not just for the children.) If you have this security, you don't have to worry. You can talk to your lawyer ahead of the scheduled appointment or find out what you need to bring to a lawyer ahead of time, so the actual visit will be less confrontational. Remember, you will have to say where all of your worldly possessions and maybe your children are headed. These are difficult topics and maybe should not be discussed for the first time in front of a stranger. The more you both know about each other's visions on your estate when you both leave it the better. Remember, you are a team and you need to discuss this topic as a team. Under most circumstances, you will each have your own will leaving your estates to each other. In most strong marriages, each spouse has a copy of the other's will and therefore knows how to manage the estate in an emergency.

Another valuable document to review with a lawyer is a Living Will. This document addresses an event that would leave you incapacitated to make your own decisions. You will want to discuss with your spouse if you choose to hold each with the responsibility of making decisions for you.

Time Value of Money: If you earn $10 today, it is worth more than $10 next year. Why? Because $10 invested today should earn you interest, and be worth more than $10 next year. So, if you start investing as a couple early for your retirement, you should have much more of a nest egg than if you start investing later in life. Enough said by me, but the two of you as a couple need to think about that concept as you are moving along in your careers and investing for your golden years.

Compounded Interest: This is where your money really starts to add up. It's basically the anti-credit card theory. In this case, interest is working in your favor on your initial deposit, as opposed to costing you at your initial purchase (like a credit card debt would).

Let's simplify this definition and say you are putting $1000 into a bank account. Your $1000 in your bank account will earn a certain interest rate over a certain period.

Let's say 3 percent annually. So, at the end of the first year, you now have $1030. At the start of the new year, you are now earning interest on that extra $30 earned in the first year as well as your initial $1000 deposit. Now, at the end of two years, you have $1030 plus an additional 3% interest on $1030, or $1060.90.

BRIDE

Retirement—To Do:
1) Do you think ahead to retirement?
2) At what age would you like to stop working?
3) What kind of lifestyle do you expect once you have retired?
4) Do you have IRA's set up?
5) Do you have 401K's or other company deferred compensation plans in place for you both?
6) Do you know how your money is allocated in each of the funds? Are you attached to certain funds? Are you willing to re-assess your own retirement plan now that you are a couple?

Wills—To Do:
1) Will you will each other everything?
   a. Who will be second in line if not children?
   b. Who will take care of the children?
2) Will you have life insurance policies?
   a. Will you create these before children?
   b. Who will be the beneficiaries?
3) Do you have thoughts on how you will set up these policies?
   a. Term or Whole Life policies for example
4) If you already have children, discuss how you financially want the children cared for within the will, as well as otherwise.

GROOM

Retirement—To Do:
1) Do you think ahead to retirement?
2) At what age would you like to stop working?
3) What kind of lifestyle do you expect once you have retired?
4) Do you have IRA's set up?
5) Do you have 401K's or other company deferred compensation plans in place for you both?
6) Do you know how you money is allocated in each of the funds? Are you attached to certain funds? Are you willing to re-assess your own retirement plan now that you are a couple?

Wills—To Do:
1) Will you will each other everything?
   a. Who will be second in line if not children?
   b. Who will take care of the children?
2) Will you have life insurance policies?
   a. Will you create these before children?
   b. Who will be the beneficiaries?
3) Do you have thoughts on how you will set up these policies?
   a. Term or Whole Life policies for example
4) If you already have children, discuss how you financially want the children cared for within the will, as well as otherwise.

XIII. Children

Discussion:

Children can be the icing on a great couples partnership. They can make you laugh, cry, and do some fairly ridiculous things all in the name of love. That said, children are never the band-aid to a partnership, and they are not free. They are labor intensive, financially costly, and require tons of communication by parents to make the partnership run smoothly and keep the child clueless as to all that is going on around them related to their presence.

Many religious organizations ask where you see yourself, and with how many children certain years into the marriage. This is an important question. However, what many organizations fail to ask, and I hope this chapter can, are questions related to being financially responsible for the children. As a team, you should discuss how you plan to take care of the children.

Now, do not take this as saying the honeymoon is over. It can be quite fun to plan into your future, and think about where you will be ten years from now. Look at this exercise as seeing into the future and trying to understand where you want to be with raising the children. You can try to see if you are being practical or just romantic about your hopes and dreams. For those of you with all the money in the world, this exercise is more about where you see yourself with your career goals once you have children. Is the constant care going to be from you and you need to re-assess the chapter on "Professional Careers" in this book? From family and friends? Or are you going to be the sequel to "The Nanny Diaries"?

Speaking of nannies and outside child care, as a couple you should decide how you want to take care of this child when it comes to care outside the home. Childcare can be expensive. As I write this book, a typical cost quote for full time care for one child per week in day care is approximately $300. Of course, this will vary based on where you live. But, in general, you get the idea. Bright Horizons Family Solutions has a web site at www.brighthorizons.com that addresses many day care solutions. You may be able to find phone numbers and contacts of centers near you to call to find out what competitive rates are for day care when it is time. This is not a job for one parent, it is a long and arduous task to figure out the place you are most comfortable sending your child, so do not hope that one click and three cost quotes will finish your search. But it is a start when your time comes.

Part-time:

Neither of you may want to totally leave your careers just yet. Consider yourselves lucky. You both feel that satisfaction from your work day that comes from making a difference. However, what you also should be aware of is that now, with this really great child, one of you may decide to cut down on your professional workload. If that happens, a whole new budget will have to be drafted. You have to start all over again. But think of all of this new work ahead of you as just that—A New Beginning for your relationship.

What you should think about is how friendly your employer is to part time schedules, new mother's choices to nurse and to pick up their baby from day care on-time, and new father's choices to take responsibility for doctor's appointments and baseball game schedules. Some companies support their employees fully, others look for every window to ask employees to leave if they cannot hack the fast lane anymore. Discussing your company values with your spouse may put you into a position where you are looking for a new job that is stable and family-friendly before you have the new bundle of joy in your arms. Future planning is not a crime. Discussing how your employer is treating new parents should not be either. It is a touchy subject sometimes, but you should be prepared. Are you ready to leave your career if your company will not have you back part-time? Is your spouse ready to leave the daily grind? Are there other new companies and fresh careers out there that you want to get established in prior to having a child? I know I am always shocked when I see the lack of support by companies to keep new parents employed part time until they are potentially ready to commit full time again. Be prepared and work on this financial project together.

Investment Choices:

There have been some new breakthroughs in helping parents save to put their children through college, if your child chooses that path. There are plans that have been developed in states to help parents save on a tax-deferred basis. These are called 529 Plans and are constantly being improved to help families save for a child's college education. For more information, you should look on your own states web site for information about your states individual plan. For example, the state of Connecticut has an excellent web site at www.aboutchet.com that can answer the basic questions for you about these 529 college savings plans. There is also a calculator that assesses information you input on current college costs to help you calculate the finances that will be needed for the four years of college. The great piece about state plans at this time is that you are not pigeonholed into only investing into your own state's plan. You are welcome to research any state's plan you see that you think has the best investments for you, and invest there. When you are researching your plans you may notice that there are options in how you want to invest your money in the college savings plan. For example, your state may offer a plan with a high equity option that invests much of the money in growth and income funds. You may also be offered a plan that guarantees your principal that you put into the plan, but only guarantees a modest gain with potential for slightly more. You may also be offered the investment option of a managed allocation fund. This fund starts out investing in higher risk options, but becomes more conservative as you come closer to needing the money to be guaranteed. These choices all go back to you both as a couple sitting down and discussing how risk averse you are when it comes to investing in your child's college education plan. But this is not a discussion that should happen when your child is fifteen years old, it should happen when your child is fifteen months old. You need time to think about these options and to change your mind until you are comfortable with the final decision. Good luck with the future of your little one.

Since we have already noted that indeed children are awesome, but need financial backing, here are some discussion questions for you and your partner to dwell on. None of the questions below should be the question that makes you think you should not have those little people. Instead, these questions just help you in better understanding your financial situation once you have made the decision to have children.

BRIDE

To Do:
1) If you decide to have children, will you set up an educational fund for them?
   a. At what age will the child be when will you start this fund?
   b. How much money will you set aside to this fund?
   c. How often will you make deposits to this fund?
   d. How faithful do you plan to be to this fund? (For example, is this the first fund or the last fund to be ignored when bills are high in a month?)
2) Do you believe your children should put themselves through school?
3) Will you set up a trust fund for your child? At what age will you release it to him/her?
4) If you both decide to continue to work, have you thought about how you will keep the children happy while you are at work? What kind of day care would you consider and what costs would you be willing to spend on these day care options?

GROOM

To Do:

1) If you decide to have children, will you set up an educational fund for them?
   a. At what age will the child be when will you start this fund?
   b. How much money will you set aside to this fund?
   c. How often will you make deposits to this fund?
   d. How faithful do you plan to be to this fund? (For example, is this the first fund or the last fund to be ignored when bills are high in a month?)
2) Do you believe your children should put themselves through school?
3) Will you set up a trust fund for your child? At what age will you release it to him/her?
4) If you both decide to continue to work, have you thought about how you will keep the children happy while you are at work? What kind of day care would you consider and what costs would you be willing to spend on the day care options?

XIV. A Summary—The Final Exam.

Discussion:
Hopefully this book has helped you both to answer some financial questions about you as a new couple in a fun and non-threatening environment for the two of you. Some topics will be more important to you than others at different stages in your lives as you move through your marriage. As with everything else in marriage, your financial status will constantly be in flux as you grow as people and make changes in your lives.

Every part of marriage holds surprises, and financial decisions are no exception. Making the decisions together bonds you together as a couple. Trouble starts when the communication stops. So, remember your CASH. Never forget that the person sitting across the table from you as you discuss your latest financial challenge is the person you love more than anyone else. If you keep in mind that you never want to make this person worry needlessly over a financial decision that you make, then make the decision together.

Quick and Dirty Questions:
As much as you both can prepare for odd financial circumstances to occur, you cannot plan for them all. This chapter includes a few topic questions that could cause a bit of ruckus. See if your marriage could survive these times. Try to stick to this approach when tackling the questions:

1) Think about the situation independently. Write down exactly how you would respond to the circumstance. Be honest, there are no extra points for thinking ahead to what your partner will say and matching that answer.

2) Share your independent answers with each other.

3) Negotiate with each other what the final resolution will be. Would you really decide that one partner's answer was better than the other, or would the final answer be somewhere in between. This last piece of this project is always the toughest. Since it is not real life, it can also still be fun.

Partner Point: An important point while you are doing these exercises is to see how you feel when you bring forward your ideas to your partner. Think about how you feel about your contribution, and how you feel about your partner's contribution. Are you embarrassed by your contribution? Do you totally depend on your partner? Do you think your partner does not have a clue and your answer is absolute? Are you communicating your concerns seriously to your partner? This is the time to realize that you cannot add zero percent to the decisions that occur in your home, nor can you add one hundred per cent. So work at it now, with these Quick and Dirty Questions before it becomes a real life problem later.

BRIDE

To Do:

Question #1:
You have saved $500 from overtime work that you have put in. How do you manage that money? (i.e. savings account, splurge on the couple, splurge on yourself, invest in a stable investment, invest in a risky investment)

Questions #2:
You have your family and your husband's family. How much, prior to becoming a couple, did you spend on family at the holidays? How much will you spend now? (It is important here to note if the price tag is unimportant to you.)

Questions #3:
You are given $10,000 at your wedding. How do you manage it?

Question #4:
You have consistently given $X/year to you favorite charity. You are now part of a partnership. Your husband gives $Y/year to his favorite charity. How, if at all, will this change? Discuss your beliefs on donations to charities and how you would like that to change (or not to change) once you are a couple.

Question #5:
You have had your favorite car for eight years. Sadly, it is just time to give it up and get a new one. What car do you buy? What role in the decision does your husband play?

Question #6
You have a list of upcoming events to attend. One birthday party with your family, one cocktail party with your friends, one sporting event with your husband's friends, one college bash with some of his friends and some of your friends and one holiday party with his family. You can't do it all, how do you prioritize among your family, your husband's family, your friends, and your husband's friends? For which of the events do you have financial burdens placed on you? Do you buy gifts for all of the events? If so, what price tag do you put on such events? Are there other events your husband may not know have a price tag associated with them?

Question #7:
You have a new place to live. There is much expensive work to do. How do you both feel about investing in the home?
    Structural issues (new windows and doors, new attic stairs, etc.)
    Gardening issues (mowing, weeding, planting)

If you are both busy, what type of investment do you plan on making in having others do the weekly / monthly upkeep to the home?

Question #8:
You are at a large picnic with family and friends. Someone asks you a financial question. Will you answer this question? Or, will you keep your new family financial issues between the two of you private? Have you discussed between the two of you what financial issues stay within the couple and what can be discussed at this picnic and other social event with the world listening?

Question #9:
You just had a baby. Up until you had the child, you thought you absolutely would continue working starting eight weeks after having the baby, and told your Director as much as you left for the hospital. Now you have the baby in your arms and can't imagine going back. Your mind has changed on a very major topic in a very short time. How will you and your spouse handle that immediate change? Discuss that both on the level of financial issues to be re-considered and on the level of communicating with each other about the changes that need to happen now that there will only be one income in the home.

Question #10:
You have some basic needs that you had when you were single, and plan on continuing now that you are a couple. Does your husband know what these are? (For example, season tickets to football games or the opera, trips to the spa, your weekly book club)

In general, how do you manage the money that is spent individually on each of you? Do you have an equal allowance for each of you to spend as you wish on a monthly basis? Or, do you have financial allowances according to your salaries? Or, do you not track what you spend on these splurges, since you had them before, they should stay the same now.

GROOM

To Do:

Question #1:
You have saved $500 from overtime work that you have put in. How do you manage that money? (I.e. savings account, splurge on the couple, splurge on yourself, invest in a stable investment, invest in a risky investment)

Questions #2:
You have your family and your wife's family. How much, prior to becoming a couple, did you spend on family at the holidays? How much will you spend now? (It is important here to note if the price tag is unimportant to you.)

Questions #3:
You are given $10,000 at your wedding. How do you manage it?

Question #4:
You have consistently given $X/year to you favorite charity. You are now part of a partnership. Your wife gives $Y/year to her favorite charity. How, if at all, will this change? Discuss your beliefs on donations to charities and how you would like that to change (or not to change) once you are a couple.

Question #5:
You have had your favorite car for eight years. Sadly, it is just time to give it up and get a new one. What car do you buy? What role in the decision does your wife play?

Question #6:
You have a list of upcoming events to attend. One birthday party with your family, one cocktail party with your friends, one sporting event with your wife's friends, one college bash with some of her friends and some of your friends and one holiday party with her family. You can't do it all, how do you prioritize among your family, your wife's family, your friends, and your wife's friends? For which of the events do you have financial burdens placed on you? Do you buy gifts for all of the events? If so, what price tag do you put on such events? Are there other events your wife may not know have a price tag associated with them?

Question #7:
You have a new place to live. There is much expensive work to do. How do you both feel about investing in the home?
Structural issues (new windows and doors, new attic stairs, etc.)
Gardening issues (mowing, weeding, planting)

If you are both busy, what type of investment do you plan on making in having others do the weekly / monthly upkeep to the home?

Question #8:

You are at a large picnic with family and friends. Someone asks you a financial question. Will you answer this question? Or, will you keep your new family financial issues between the two of you private? Have you discussed between the two of you what financial issues stay within the couple and what can be discussed at this picnic and other social event with the world listening?

Question #9:

Your wife just had a baby. Up until she had the child, you thought she would absolutely continue working starting eight weeks after having the baby, and told her Director as much as she left for the hospital. Now you both have the baby in your arms and can't imagine your wife going back to work and bringing the baby to daycare. Your mind has changed on a very major topic in a very short time. How will you and your wife handle that immediate change? Discuss that both on the level of financial issues to be re-considered and on the level of communicating with each other about the changes that need to happen now that there will only be one income in the home.

Question #10:

You have some basic needs that you had when you were single, and plan on continuing now that you are a couple. Does your wife know what these are? (For example, season tickets to football games or the opera, trips to the spa, or your weekly book club)

In general, how do you manage the money that is spent individually on each of you? Do you have an equal allowance for each of you to spend as you wish on a monthly basis? Or, do you have financial allowances according to your salaries? Or, do you not track what you spend on these splurges, since you had them before, they should stay the same now.